Some Things Push and Some Things Pull

Alan Trussell-Cullen

Dominie Press, Inc.

Publisher: Christine Yuen
Series Editors: Adria F. Klein & Alan Trussell-Cullen
Editor: Bob Rowland
Designer: Gary Hamada

Photo Credits: Geoff Moon (Page 12); SuperStock (pages 4, 6, and 10): and Simon Young (pages 8, 14, 16, 18, and 19).

Copyright ©2001 Dominie Press, Inc. All rights reserved. No part of this publication may be reproduced or transmitted in any form or by any means without permission in writing from the publisher. Reproduction of any part of this book, through photocopy, recording, or any electronic or mechanical retrieval system, without the written permission of the publisher, is an infringement of the copyright law.

Published by:

Dominie Press, Inc.

1949 Kellogg Avenue
Carlsbad, California 92008 USA

www.dominie.com

ISBN 0-7685-0554-2

Printed in Singapore

15 16 17 18 V0ZF 13

Table of Contents

Things That Push   4
Things That Pull   8
We Push and Pull, Too!   14
Picture Glossary   20
Index   20

The bulldozer pushes the dirt.

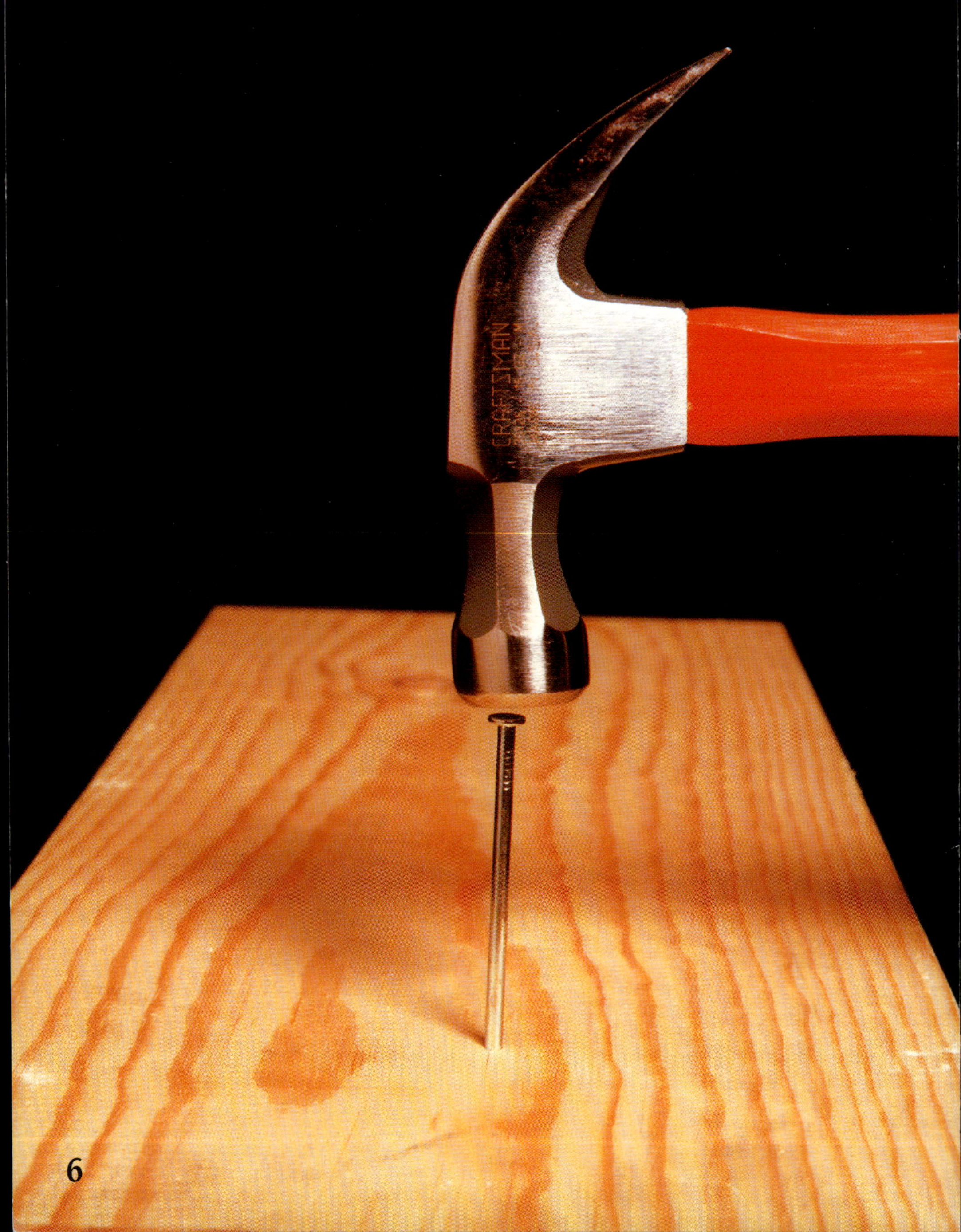
CRAFTSMAN

The hammer pushes the nail into the wood.

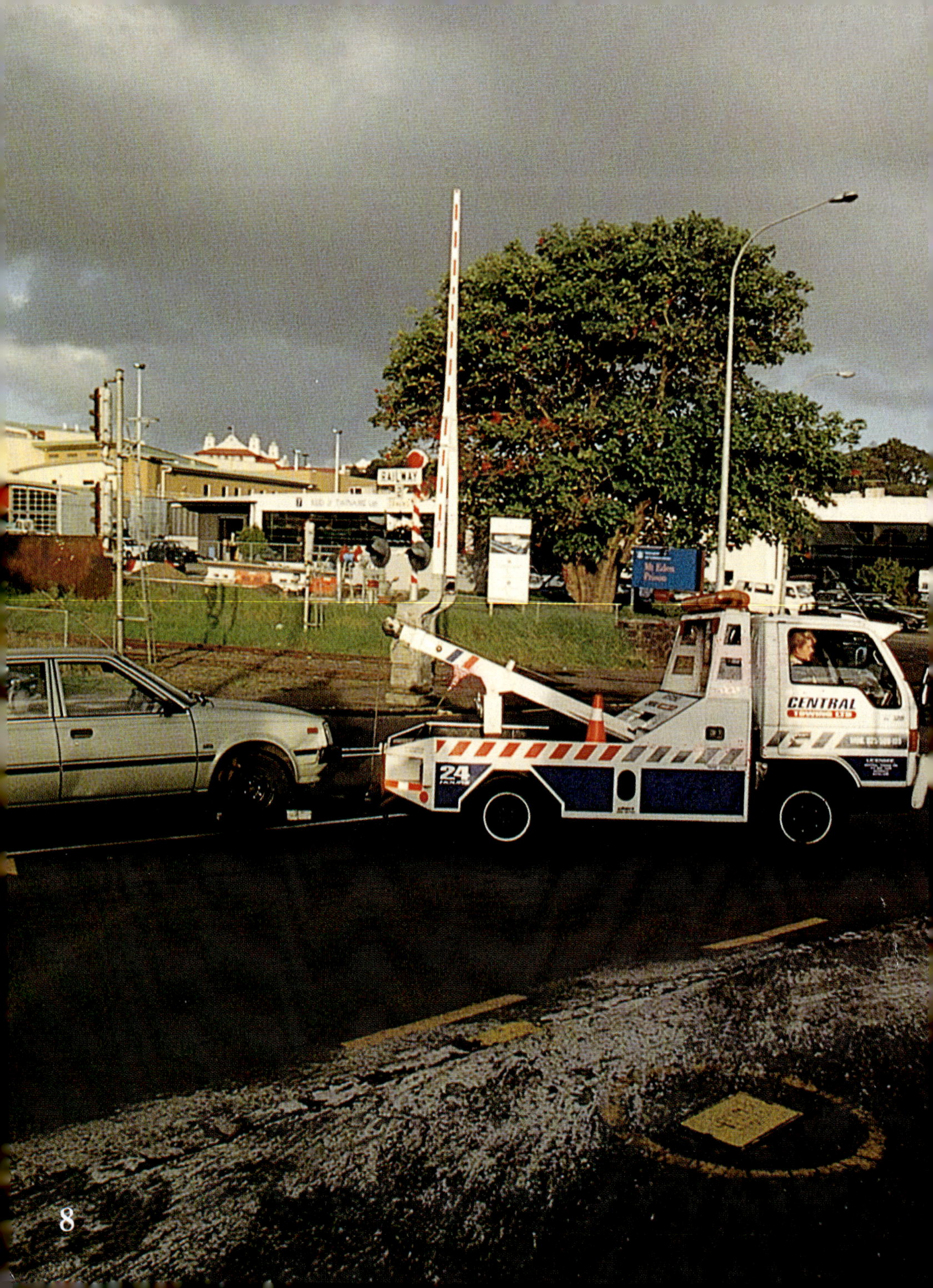
RAILWAY
Mt Eden
Prison
CENTRAL
24

The tow truck pulls the car.

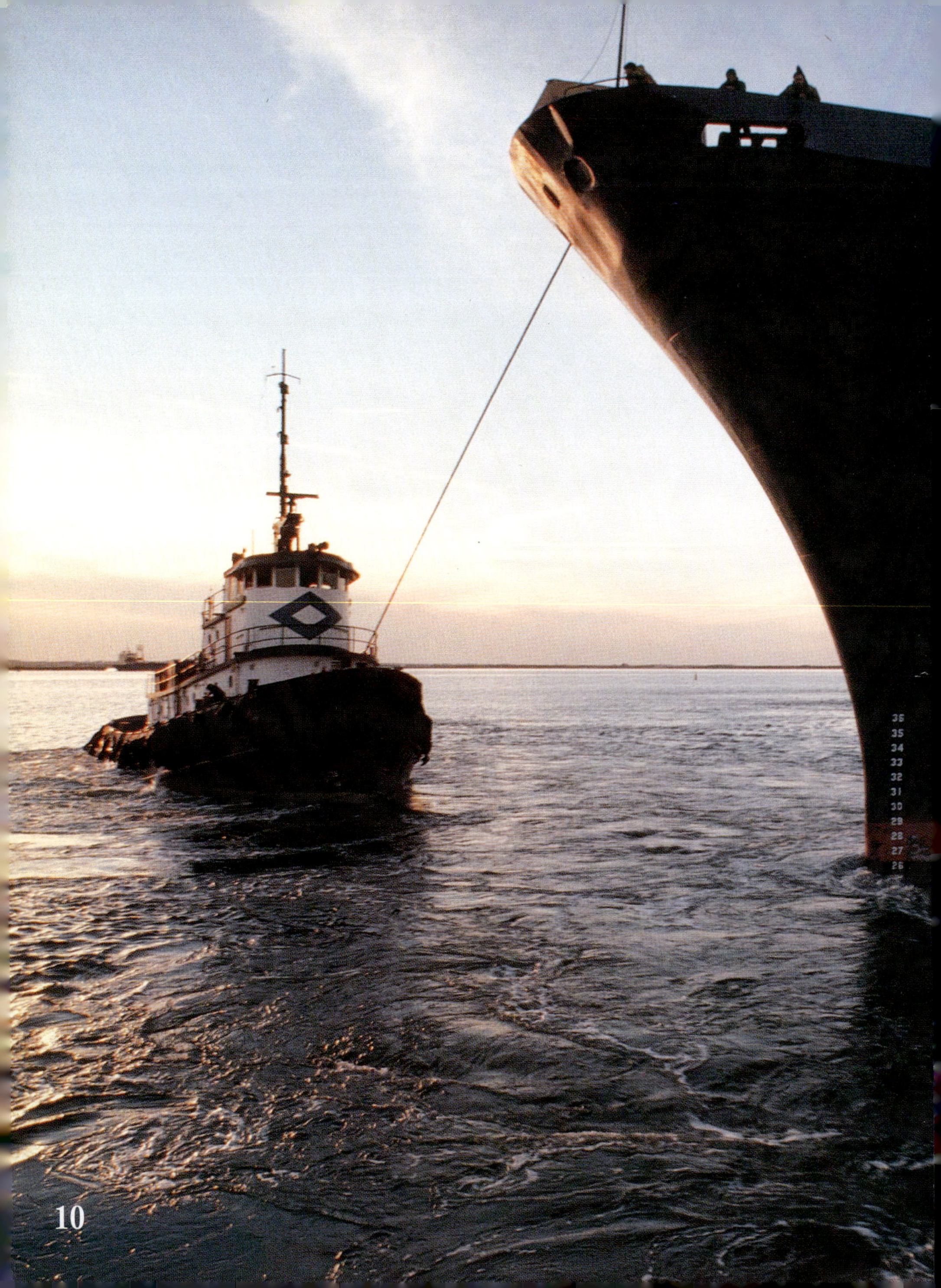

The tugboat pulls the ship.

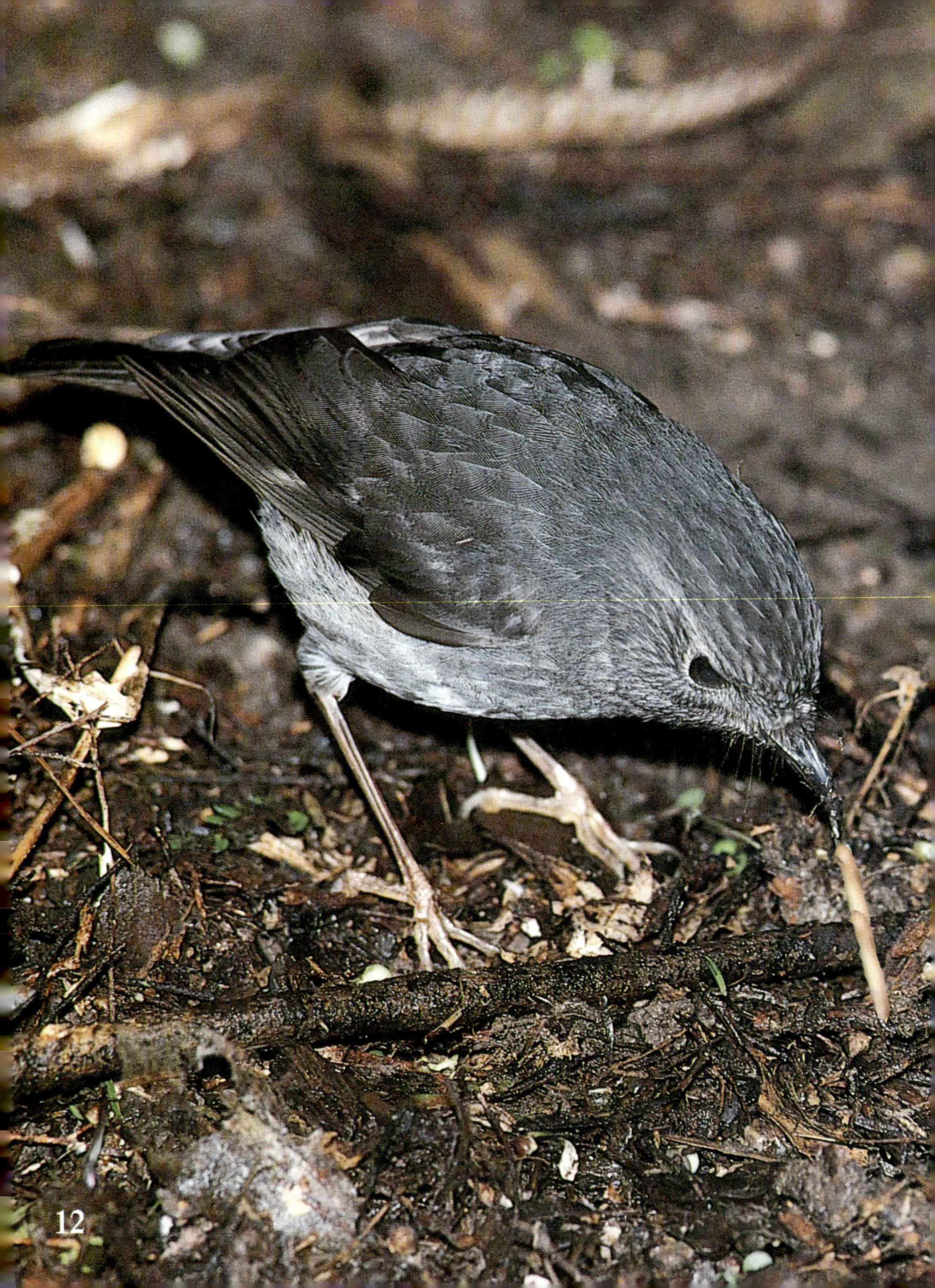

The bird pulls the worm.

14

We can push, too.

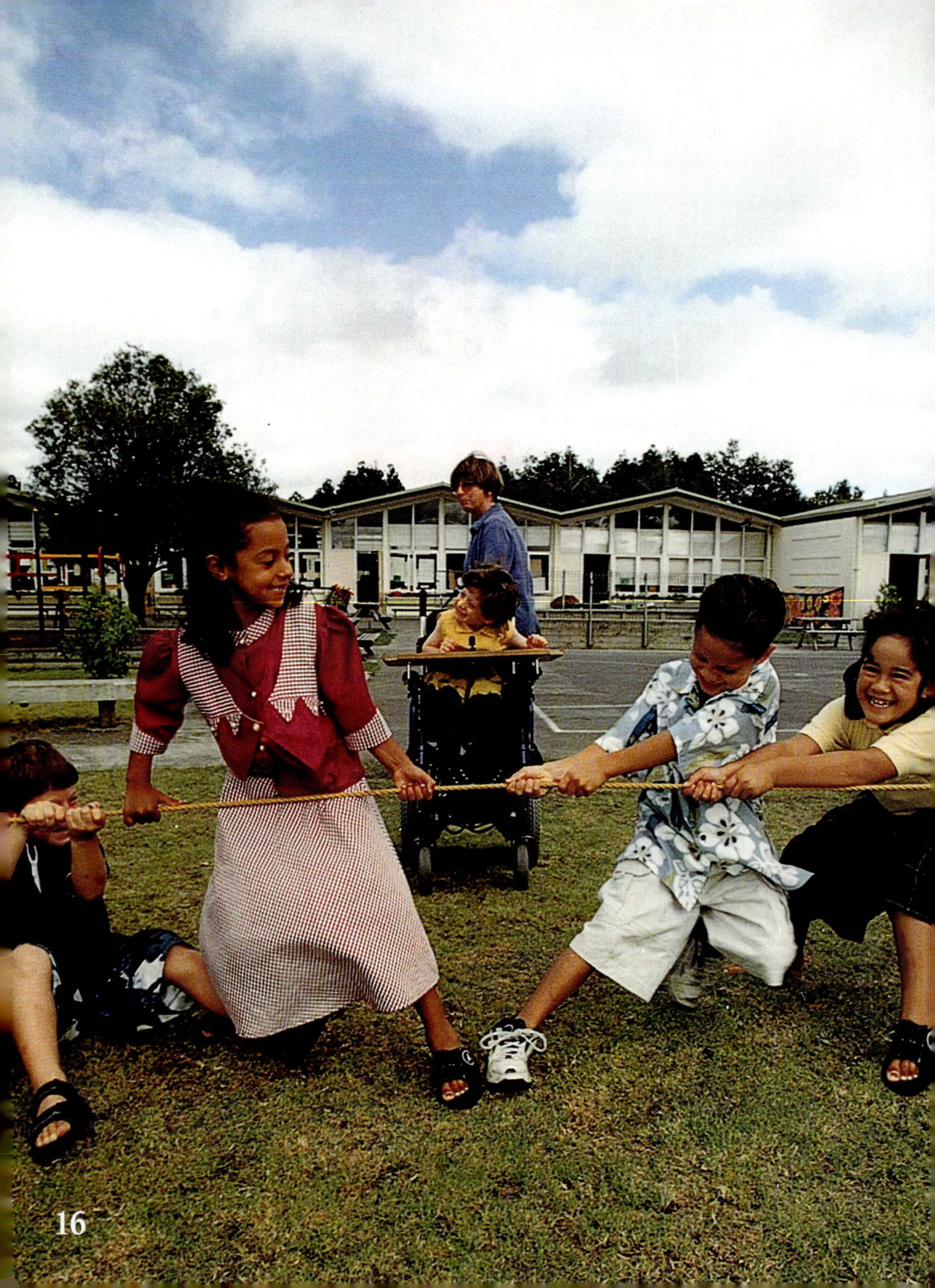

When we play tug-of-war,
we all pull!

We push some things.

Pushing the stroller - Cameron

Pushing the door closed - Liu Cheng

Pushing a goat up a hill. - Aaron

Pushing the button on a stop light - Jareden

Jack
Dad is pushing the stroller.

We pull some things.

Mathew pulling a fish.

The jet ski is pulling the water ski
Regan

Pulling a weed
- Shigh McCarthy

Reina pulling the covers over her head.

The horse is pulling a truck.
Sam

Our car pulling a trailer
- Bryan

Megan pulling a drawer.

Pulling the cord on the lawn mower
- Michael

Picture Glossary

bird:

bulldozer:

hammer:

nail:

tow truck:

tugboat:

tug-of-war:

Index

bird, 13

bulldozer, 5

hammer, 7

nail, 7

tow truck, 9

tugboat, 11

tug-of-war, 17